3/30/23
OCMCS

ENGINEERING MARVELS
PANAMA CANAL

by Vanessa Black

pogo

Ideas for Parents and Teachers

Pogo Books let children practice reading informational text while introducing them to nonfiction features such as headings, labels, sidebars, maps, and diagrams, as well as a table of contents, glossary, and index.

Carefully leveled text with a strong photo match offers early fluent readers the support they need to succeed.

Before Reading

- "Walk" through the book and point out the various nonfiction features. Ask the student what purpose each feature serves.
- Look at the glossary together. Read and discuss the words.

Read the Book

- Have the child read the book independently.
- Invite him or her to list questions that arise from reading.

After Reading

- Discuss the child's questions. Talk about how he or she might find answers to those questions.
- Prompt the child to think more. Ask: Imagine the Panama Canal was never built. How would you design a shortcut between the Atlantic and Pacific oceans? Think of as many ways as you can. Be creative!

Pogo Books are published by Jump!
5357 Penn Avenue South
Minneapolis, MN 55419
www.jumplibrary.com

Library of Congress Cataloging-in-Publication Data

Names: Black, Vanessa, 1973- author.
Title: Panama Canal / by Vanessa Black.
Description: Minneapolis, MN: Jump!, Inc., [2017]
Series: Engineering marvels | Audience: Ages 7-10.
Includes bibliographical references and index.
Identifiers: LCCN 2017007366 (print)
LCCN 2017012556 (ebook)
ISBN 9781624965814 (e-book)
ISBN 9781620317044 (hard cover: alk. paper)
Subjects: LCSH: Canals–Panama–Design and construction–History–Juvenile literature.
Panama Canal (Panama)–Design and construction–History–Juvenile literature.
Canal Zone–History–Juvenile literature.
Classification: LCC F1569.C2 (ebook)
LCC F1569.C2 B53 2017 (print) | DDC 627/.130972875–dc23
LC record available at https://lccn.loc.gov/2017007366

Editor: Kirsten Chang
Book Designer: Molly Ballanger
Photo Researcher: Molly Ballanger

Photo Credits: Dennis MacDonald/SuperStock, cover; Federico Rostagno/Shutterstock, 1; Kathy Tuite/EyeEm/Getty, 3; Dan Thornberg/Shutterstock, 4; age fotostock/SuperStock, 5; dani3315/Shutterstock, 6-7; Planet Observer/Getty, 8-9; Encyclopaedia Britannica/Getty, 10; mircea dobre/Shutterstock, 11; Ammit/Alamy, 12-13; Everett Historical/Shutterstock, 14; WILL & DENI MCINTYRE/Getty, 15; Jim Lipschutz/Shutterstock, 16-17; tose/Shutterstock, 18-19; Chris Jenner/Shutterstock, 20-21; LovePHY/Shutterstock, 23.

Printed in the United States of America at Corporate Graphics in North Mankato, Minnesota.

TABLE OF CONTENTS

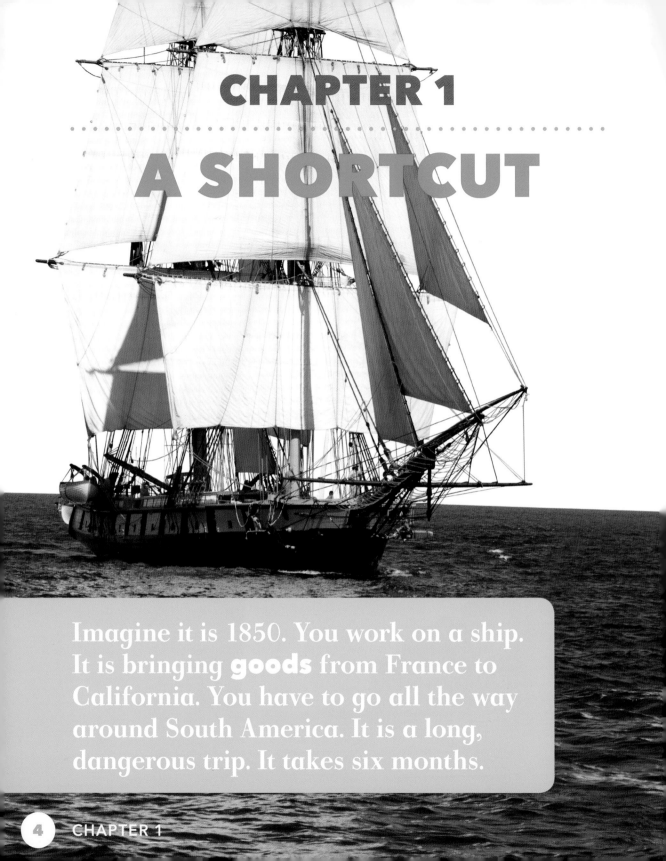

CHAPTER 1

···

A SHORTCUT

Imagine it is 1850. You work on a ship. It is bringing **goods** from France to California. You have to go all the way around South America. It is a long, dangerous trip. It takes six months.

Now imagine this trip today.
It takes just a few weeks.
Why? There is a shortcut.
The Panama **Canal**!

The Panama Canal allows ships to pass between the Atlantic and Pacific oceans. This improves trade routes all over the world. It cuts 8,000 nautical miles (15,000 kilometers) off a boat trip from New York to California. About 14,000 ships use the canal every year.

WHERE IS IT?

The Panama Canal cuts between North and South America.
It is about 50 miles (80 km) long.

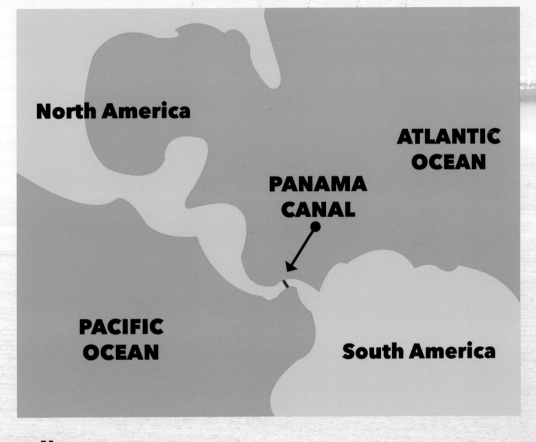

North America

ATLANTIC
OCEAN

PANAMA
CANAL

PACIFIC
OCEAN

South America

N
W — E
S

The Panama Canal opened in 1914. But it was 33 years in the making. It started with a first attempt by France in 1881. Why did they choose Panama? The land was narrow there.

Panama

CHAPTER 2

A FAILED PLAN

France planned to dig a canal at **sea level**. It had to be wide enough for ships to pass through.

THE ISTHMUS OF PANAMÁ.

Route of Canal shown thus,

0   5   10   20
English Miles.

0 5 10   20
Kilometers.   30

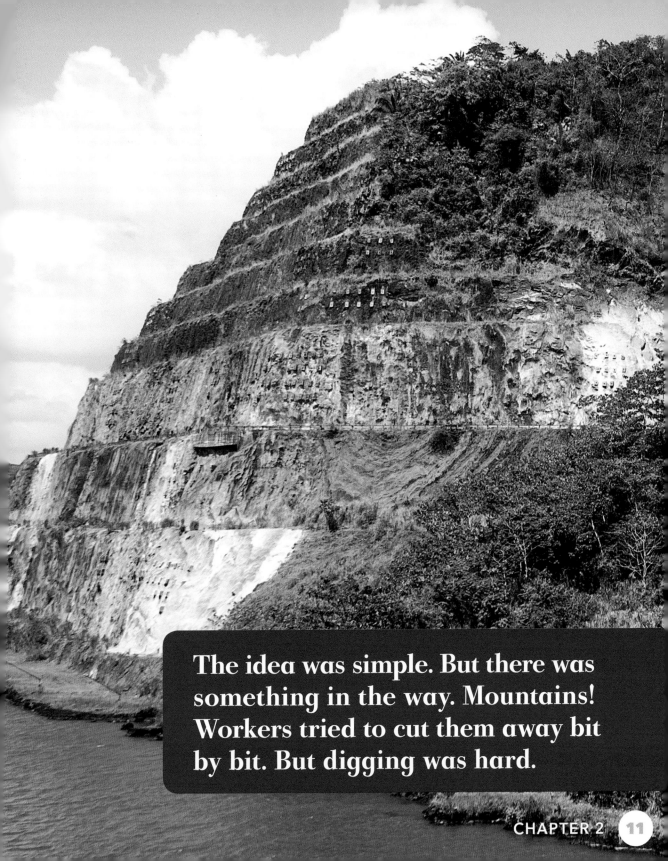

The idea was simple. But there was something in the way. Mountains! Workers tried to cut them away bit by bit. But digging was hard.

They would dig. It would rain. A **landslide** would bury their work.

Mosquitoes were another problem. They carried **disease**. Thousands of workers died. After eight years, the French gave up. They went home.

CHAPTER 3

THE SECOND PLAN

In 1904, the United States started where France left off. At first they had the same problems. But then **engineers** came up with a new plan. This plan would require less digging. It would cause fewer landslides.

Gatún Lake

First, they built **dams**. This made a large **artificial** lake at the highest point of the land. It is called Gatún Lake. Ships would pass through the lake at 85 feet (26 meters), rather than at sea level.

lock · · · · ▶

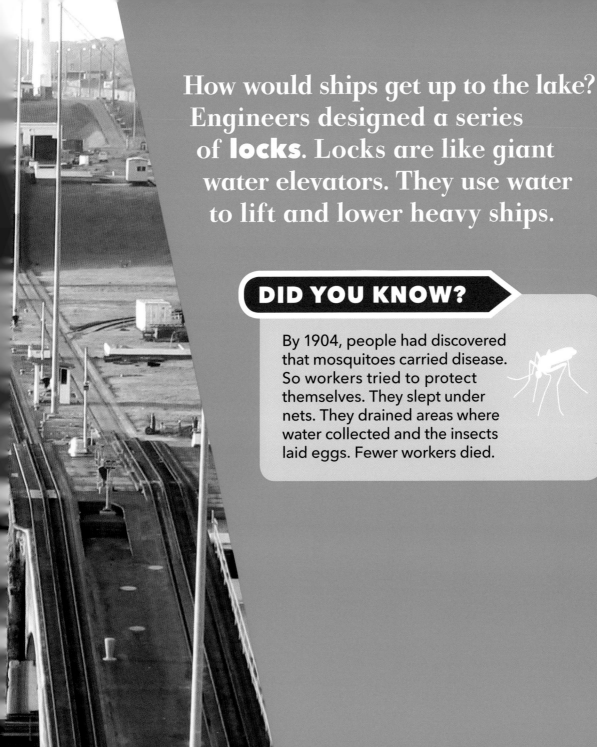

How would ships get up to the lake? Engineers designed a series of **locks**. Locks are like giant water elevators. They use water to lift and lower heavy ships.

DID YOU KNOW?

By 1904, people had discovered that mosquitoes carried disease. So workers tried to protect themselves. They slept under nets. They drained areas where water collected and the insects laid eggs. Fewer workers died.

Locks were not new. But they had never been built this big. Workers used a lot of **concrete**. How much? About 120 million cubic feet (3.4 million cubic meters)!

TAKE A LOOK!

How do locks help ships cross the Panama Canal?

❶ A ship enters the first lock at sea level. Water is pumped into the lock. This raises the ship to the level of the next lock.

❷ This is repeated until the ship is as high as the lake. It crosses the lake.

❸ It enters the first exit lock. Water is drained from the lock. This lowers the ship to the level of the next lock.

❹ This is repeated until the ship is back at sea level.

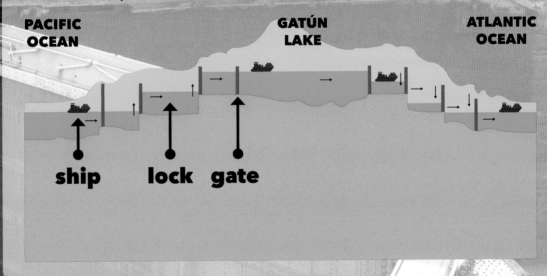

PACIFIC OCEAN

GATÚN LAKE

ATLANTIC OCEAN

ship   lock   gate

The Panama Canal opened in 1914. It was the biggest project of its day. Since that time, ships have gotten bigger. Panama recently spent five billion dollars expanding the canal. It took 10 years. It opened in 2016. It still makes us marvel!

DID YOU KNOW?

Ships have to pay **tolls** to use the canal. They pay by weight. A man swam through the canal once. He paid 36 cents.

ACTIVITIES & TOOLS

MAKE A LANDSLIDE

Landslides made it impossible for the French workers to dig the Panama Canal. Recreate the circumstances that cause a landslide. How does a landslide affect construction?

What You Need:

- dirt
- gardening trowel
- large box or plastic tub
- watering can
- water

❶ Make a mountain out of dirt. If you are inside, put it in a box or plastic tub.

❷ Start digging a canal through it.

❸ Is the mountain stable? Or does it start to fall?

❹ Now fill the watering can with water.

❺ Make it "rain" on the mountain. What happens? Does a landslide occur?

Digging a canal is not easy. Landslides happen due to instability in the earth. They also occur when it rains.

GLOSSARY

artificial: Fake.

canal: A long, narrow passage that is filled with water so boats can travel through.

concrete: A mixture of cement, sand, rocks, and water that is used in building things.

dams: Structures that stop a river from flowing, creating a lake.

disease: An illness.

engineers: People who use math and science to solve society's problems and design things humans use.

goods: Items for sale.

landslide: When a large quantity of soil, trees, and rocks falls suddenly down a slope.

locks: Areas in a canal that have gates on each end. They open and close to control the level of water.

sea level: The average level of the ocean; it is measured as zero.

tolls: Money that has to be paid to use a crossing like a bridge or a canal.

INDEX

TO LEARN MORE

Learning more is as easy as 1, 2, 3.

1) Go to www.factsurfer.com

2) Enter "PanamaCanal" into the search box.

3) Click the "Surf" button to see a list of websites.

With factsurfer, finding more information is just a click away.